How to Influence People

Learn How to Win People Over And Get Them to Say "Yes!"

Kevin Bradnik

Copyright © 2016 Kevin Bradnik

All rights reserved.

ISBN: 1540897079
ISBN-13: 978-1540897077

© Copyright 2016 by Kevin Bradnik - All rights reserved.

This document is geared towards providing exact and reliable information in regards to the topic and issue covered. The publication is sold with the idea that the publisher is not required to render accounting, officially permitted, or otherwise, qualified services. If advice is necessary, legal or professional, a practiced individual in the profession should be ordered.

- From a Declaration of Principles which was accepted and approved equally by a Committee of the American Bar Association and a Committee of Publishers and Associations.

In no way is it legal to reproduce, duplicate, or transmit any part of this document in either electronic means or in printed format. Recording of this publication is strictly prohibited and any storage of this document is not allowed unless with written permission from the publisher. All rights reserved.

The information provided herein is stated to be truthful and consistent, in that any liability, in terms of inattention or otherwise, by any usage or abuse of any policies, processes, or directions contained within is the solitary and utter responsibility of the recipient reader. Under no circumstances will any legal responsibility or blame be held against the publisher for any reparation, damages, or monetary loss due to the information herein, either directly or indirectly.

Respective authors own all copyrights not held by the publisher.

The information herein is offered for informational purposes solely, and is universal as so. The presentation of the information is without contract or any type of guarantee assurance.

The trademarks that are used are without any consent, and the publication of the trademark is without permission or backing by the trademark owner. All trademarks and brands within this book are for clarifying purposes only and are the owned by the owners themselves, not affiliated with this document.

FOREWORD

How to Influence People is a fresh look at a subject that has been long sought after. From emperors to businessmen, all have taken a look at what it means to be influential and what it means to have allies. This is a great place to start earning mannerisms, word choices, and the type of persuasion that will help you to make better use of the 6 traits of influence. Never forget that anybody and everybody has something they can do to get them on your side. A great read for any and all, it will provide insight into working better with colleagues without changing your ways, tips on conversation and social interaction, cues that those around you will respond to like paid actors. While not delving deeply into any one subject, *How to Influence People* is an all-around guide to social and personal success through the mentality of psychology.

Using tips from some of the top psychologists in the industry, and applying tried and true methods, this collection of knowledge offers a shatter-proof foundation for a foray into exploiting mental missteps and creating unique opportunities. Learn about the various things that compute passively for others and you gain the ability to actively control them. Seize the ability to correlate thoughts into actions and make new friends - or repel old enemies. Social engagements will be easier than ever and you'll be able to get exactly what you want out of them, too.

This book will detail the intricacies that you've always wondered about and will certainly enlighten you in the best and most effective strategies to use when you're in a position of influencing someone. From equals to lesser ups, you'll be rubbing shoulders with the best of them by the time you finish your first read all the way through.

So go ahead! Give it a try. You've got nothing to lose and everything to gain, for the information in these pages is sure to unlock a hidden potential within you. It has been created to do exactly that: to unlock the suave leader figure that resides inside all of us. You already have every tool you're going to need, now; you just need to know how to utilize them. From the power of positive thinking to instilling that same feeling in another, this will truly be a great read for you.

Contents

Introduction	1
Chapter 1: Self-Influence: Body Positioning	3
Chapter 2: Social Influence: Body Positioning	7
Chapter 3: What Causes Influence?	11
Chapter 4: Reinforcement: Positive and Negative	23
Chapter 5: Styles of Influence	30
Chapter 6: A Warning	35
Chapter 7: Influence on TV and in Real Life	41
Conclusion	48
Free Preview: How Analyzing People Helps you	51
Successful People are already Aware of this Power:	52
Anyone can Learn this Skill:	53
What are the Consequences of not Learning this?	53
How to Approach this Information:	55
It's about Knowledge, not Judgment:	57

INTRODUCTION

Congratulations on buying *How to Influence People* and thank you for doing so.

The most successful businessmen in the history of Mankind have long been attributed with success and glory. These men and women didn't make it on their natural charisma alone - they acquired charisma. Though such a feat seems unlikely, the "acquisition" of likable traits and the discarding of any traits that are, in general, socially unacceptable, is not terribly hard. When people think of successful, albeit and "crazy" businessmen, the two most commonly thought of people are Steve Jobs, of Apple fame, and Patrick Bateman, the protagonist of the critically acclaimed movie *American Psycho.* You won't have to become a psycho to win over people with charm and wit; that's all fantasy. It's as easy as learning what to do, how to do it, and putting it to the test in life real social situations.

Introduction

The following chapters will discuss the importance and meaning of how your body is positioned, both to yourself and to others, the key tools of influence, along with the methods through which you will influence people. It also takes a look at some common mistakes that can jeopardize your plans or ruin relationships entirely, and helps you to avoid them by simply knowing they exist. Finally, we go over the real and true ways that you will influence people and give you a few tips on fitting in to new environments.

The author knows that there are plenty of books on this subject on the market and wants to thank you again for choosing this one! A great amount of time and effort was put into making this an enjoyable and informative experience, and I hope that you learn everything you sought to! Read on, ye curious souls, and find out exactly *How to Influence People*!

Chapter 1: Self-Influence: Body Positioning

One thing that should be made known immediately is that in order for any of the provided information to be effective, one has to believe that it will be so. Doubt is a natural reaction to just about anything that seems new, foreign, or unlikely; but through confidence, it becomes easy to see the fruits of one's labor.

For some, however, it isn't a matter of an active state of mind. Worrying is passive; it's a natural reaction to everything. There's good news for all the worry-warts of the world, though: You can dispel this worry with a few easy and simple tips.

Allow for a moment of clarity here: Telling yourself things like "don't worry," or "stop being afraid" is not the way to go. Repeating things over and over, like a mantra in your head, will not have positive effects; it will instead create a zone of negativity. You know that you're afraid of what's to come, and

Chapter 1: Self-Influence: Body Positioning

you're using the least effective method of stilling yourself against it.

So what's one to do? Firstly, don't think of anything at all. Clear your mind as best you can, and just focus. Look around you, but not too far out. How are you stood or seated? If you're sitting with your legs closed, hands in your lap, and chin to your chest, you're doing it wrong. If you're standing with arms crossed over your chest or hands in your pockets, with legs stuck together like a toy army soldier, again, that's not going to help you at all.

The way you stand is essential to the way you think. Your positioning, meaning your posture, the position of your hands, and even where your feet are pointing can dictate a lot about your thought processes. If you stand small, with your feet together and your shoulders humped forward, eyes pointed down, your thoughts will roam to negative places.

Positive thinking isn't about mental capacity alone, it's about the passive cues that your body gives to your mind. When space allows, stand with your feet spread about the distance of your shoulders, and your shoulders should be straight out. Your arms can remain at your sides if you keep your shoulders squared, but when possible, raise them behind your head or connect them at the hands on the small of your back. This positioning takes up more space than usual, but can help you to think positively. A good posture not only looks good from the outside, but can empower your thinking on the inside.

This adjustment of one's body can be incredibly potent, and is often called "power positioning." The entire idea revolves around your posture, affecting the way you think. If you make yourself large and wide, by spreading apart your arms or legs or puffing out your chest, your mind will project differently than if you sit bundled up, hands in your pockets or tucked under your arms--and that difference is normally a positive one.

Positioning yourself is not only something you do for your own mental benefit, however. The way you stand does not go unnoticed - which is the reason why power positioning works differently in social situations. When speaking with other people, it is important not to stand out too obviously.

CHAPTER 1: SELF-INFLUENCE: BODY POSITIONING

Chapter 2: Social Influence: Body Positioning

The importance of knowing what others think when they stand near you is important to influencing them and predicting what they're thinking about you. Being able to know what others are thinking about you is knowledge of how best to approach a situation involving them.

Traditionally, when speaking with a group of people, a circle normally forms. This circle can be manipulated, and it is normally done passively. However, knowing how to mimic these passive actions is key to influencing the situation.

The primary manipulation techniques involve pushing people out of the circle or trying to draw them in closer. To do this, you need to be able to send signals, both discouraging and reinforcing. This is all about eyes, feet, and directions.

Firstly, know the importance of your feet. Traditionally, in a healthy circle of conversation, everybody's feet get pointed toward the center, or maybe pointed in the direction of their favorite speaker. If you wish to remove somebody from the circle, the best way to go about this is to turn your back on them, literally. If you move your feet to point away from them, you'll isolate them from the circle. If you can get other people in the circle to do the same, all the better.

Your visual search pattern is also important in social circles. You'll normally look directly at the speaker as they do their thing; however, if you ignore a speaker by not making eye contact, or react negatively to what they say, they will eventually feel uncomfortable enough to leave the circle.

Of course, facial expressions mean the world here, but don't be overly aggressive. Frowning or scowling at somebody you want out of a social circle will be strange. Neutral or unresponsive reactions will be more than enough to discourage unwelcome speakers.

The opposite is easy enough to achieve as well. You can positively reinforce speakers by looking at them, preferably through eye contact and smiling at them as they speak. Laughter, physical contact via hands on shoulders or playful nudges are also encouraging. Keep the conversation lighthearted and fun to provide a welcoming aura, or try and keep voices low and the circle tight to constrict it to the current people conversing.

In public situations, it is wise to hold your ground even during a rough patch. You will not always have the support of the social circle. They may passively be fighting against you, to keep certain people in or out of the conversation. As long as you can tell that their cues are passive, and you maintain your active ones, you should come out ahead in the end.

These situations work best standing next to whomever it is you're trying to influence in the circle. To work your way over to them, first you have to leave the circle briefly. Get a drink or a snack and bring it back to the circle, now standing next to the person you want to encourage or discourage. Favor them by facing towards them or disregard them by turning away.

Social situations are not always so easy, though. Sometimes, these circles aren't established. Chairs, tables, or other conveniences might project a conversation over a greater distance, and set a finite number of people who can comfortably chat. Assuming a formal situation, say, a wedding after party or business gathering, you will have to be careful not to overexert yourself when not in a circle. Sometimes it's as easy as sitting in one of the seats; other times, it takes taking somebody out of the conversation even temporarily to nab their seats.

At a formal dining event, such actions cannot be taken. Isolation and removal from conversations is not a possibility. Instead, working damage control is the best that can be done.

If another person is attempting to discredit you in some way, do not sink to their level. Remain above it and merely deflect their claims. Do not say anything against the other person, simply remain civil. Eventually, they will tire of it. If they have something real and are attracting attention, do your best to either discredit their words, or simply refuse to respond.

If you need the effect of power positioning while in a conversation, attempt to maintain subtlety. Stretching can help achieve this, allowing you to stealthily increase the space you occupy. Stepping away and coming back afterwards will allow you to adopt a new stance that helps to keep you feeling confident. Hands on hips, or behind your back, are both ways that help you to briefly maintain such a position.

Chapter 3: What Causes Influence?

The Six Factors

It is often generalized that there are six factors that contribute to the willingness of a person to allow themselves to be influenced by words. In no particular order, they appeal to the level of authority one has, how good a friend they are, if any favors are owed, if it allows them to be consistent, if it would allow them to appear popular, and if it would net them a benefit.

These things can all help you influence people, and it is best to start with authority. Often times a matter of coincidence, the authority, real or perceived, you have or lack over a person is a true game changer. Though there's little you can do about real authority that involves social situations with which you are familiar, the idea of perceived authority is more than enough to get you what you need in the face of unfamiliarity. Even when you are unable to pull rank, you can always feign superiority.

Chapter 3: What Causes Influence?

The school you went to, the education you received, the job you possess, all of this can be used to put you in a position of perceived authority--and this can be enough to influence other people.

Influencing is more than just manipulating, it's idealizing and it's cooperation. If you are well acquainted with somebody, they are much more likely to help you than a stranger would be. Strong allies allow you to be strong yourself, and getting in good with the right people, just because they like you as a person, is no doubt a great way to secure yourself the trust of another.

While requiring one to look ahead a good deal, the idea of reciprocity, or the exchanging of favors, holds a great deal of sway in the minds of others. This is a tool whose application scales contrary to usefulness, meaning that the harder something becomes to do, the less weight the idea of the favor you performed holds. If you supply the favor of helping a friend move, they are not likely to do something that is more difficult than moving homes. This means you will normally have to do more for somebody than you are expecting in return. This does not mean, however, that favors are less important than other ideas about what causes influence. Sometimes, it's all about the perception of difficulty. Tasks that would be perceived as more difficult, but are in reality much easier to perform with a specific set of skills or assistance, can mean getting more than what you actually paid for. The hefty tasks being performed often hold more purpose in name than in actual work when being brought up at a later date.

Consistency is key. This mantra is rather well known, but holds true through and through. If doing something would allow somebody to remain consistent with previous actions and costs them little to nothing, they are more likely to do it. This is both true of natural consistency and artificial consistency, meaning the way people truly act or the way they want to be perceived as acting. If somebody is trying to maintain a social illusion of some sort, they are especially likely to be swayed into being influenced, since doing otherwise could potentially ruin the guise they were building. Typically, though, if somebody does something for some particular reason, the odds are they're likely willing to a similar thing for similar reasons, be they rewards or morals.

Speaking of rewards, they normally stand out as the most well-known way to get what you want out of people due to often being the most effective. While all other forms of influence do hold merit and weight, the truest one that has lasted throughout all of history is the answer to the ancient question: "What's in it for me?" The idea that actions will be rewarded, either with physical possessions, fiat money, loyalty, or information, is the most surefire way to avoid losing influence in the minds of people. If you rely solely on consistency or reciprocity, the odds are that you will lose influence. The treasures of the vault can buy you everything that a favor could and even more than authority can often offer.

These 6 elements of influence provide a great deal of utility when recognized and understood cognitively. To fully grasp the workings of these things, knowing what they are with a conscious thought process can be a great deal of help. While the knowledge of such things is often passive, actively seizing the means to control them is an important part of knowing how to properly apply them. If a situation requires authority, it's better to understand it knowingly than having just the mere thought of it.

When working with these influential ideals, it is important to understand that they are not to be used lightly. While knowing is half the battle, proper application is the other half. It's true, you're not likely to be called out when working carefully, but if people are suspicious that you may be trying to affect their mentality, they could resist your suave advances.

The Idea of Honesty

In a perfect world, nobody would have to lie to anybody. We could all understand the shortcomings of those around us, admit our own, and be better people. This is not the world we live in, however, and, therefore, dishonesty has become another factor of life that makes it seem painful or dreadful. Since everybody else lies, there's no reason to be honest yourself, right? Unfortunately, this is true: to influence others, you will have to lie--be it compliments paid to a dress you don't particularly think looks good on the woman wearing it, or idealizing a future you don't find certain to a potential group of new influences; or in the worst case, fudging numbers and fixing data to appeal to certain higher-ups. While the author of the E-book does not condone lying, it must be said: you can't be influential with the truth alone.

But, you also can't be influential based solely on lies. If your entire social life is based on a tangled web of dishonesty, the odds are that it won't hold. Lying doesn't look good to anybody; and if one is discovered, it puts everything you say into question. To minimize the chance of being caught lying, lie less and lie smaller. If you are caught, fall back on the many moments that you told the truth, and remind everybody that what you had done, what you had covered up with information that wasn't truthful, wasn't significant. Yeah, maybe you were dishonest, but it pales in comparison to all the good things you've done. And if the lie produced a plethora of positive outcomes, hammer the point that it was for a good cause.

People like honesty. Nobody wants to be lied to. If you're as honest as you can be and avoid lying to people, it will look good. This all goes without saying, of course, but it is essential to keep in mind. Choose your words carefully and keep a noble mindset. When you lie to people, they will assume you think yourself above the truth, not simply telling a lie, but they'll be right: When you lie, you don't do it to get caught. You do it to create an illusion, one you're hoping won't be destroyed. You're putting yourself above honesty.

As a final note on honesty, you can maintain the illusion of honesty by covering the tracks of your lies. Politicians are best known for this, naturally, appearing as goodhearted, trustworthy individuals until one little thread of a scandal gets pulled and years of political deals and black-market-type offerings all come out. Businessmen are capable of the same, namely, the owners and employees of big banks before the economic crash seemed more trustworthy than they actually were, and that was because they all seemed like they were selling positivity until it all went wrong and their lies were revealed. The point here is that if you're careful, your tracks will never be found. While the life of anybody who is considered "small time" isn't glamorous, it also isn't being prodded until bursting by journalists. If you're a good enough liar, you can maintain the illusion of honesty without ever being caught.

Other Concepts of Influence

Of course, for some, working with these six factors is not a problem. It's the other means through which one normally gains influence that are the issues. Social do's and don'ts that can become misconstrued or overlooked when trying to imagine the big picture. For this, you need a few tips on things that make people not only more approachable from your end but also more willing to be approached on theirs.

Getting people to do you a favor in the first place can be a bit of a challenge. There are two well-known methods to do this, and it depend on the scale of the favor being asked. To get a large favor completed, you should build up to it by asking for smaller ones. In other words, if you need a small favor to be done, you should ask for a large favor first.

When you ask somebody for something small and they help you, they will be inclined to continue helping you with progressively larger factors. It's true, you will owe them more, but getting what you need done ought to be worth it. On the flip side, if you ask for something ludicrous and they refuse, they're more inclined to help you with something small. Now, ludicrous does not mean unrealistic - don't ask for a million dollars. But maybe you can propose that they play designated driver for a group of your drunk friends; and after they refuse, ask for the gas money that would pay for it even that's a little ridiculous. So maybe you just ask to borrow their van and pay for the gas yourself. Working your way down will help you to establish a smaller favor.

People are selfish. This is the reason why reciprocity is often rewarded with less than you originally invested. However, the fact remains that you can use it to your advantage. While the six traits of influence are all very important, they are very often wasted when people are viewed as tools and then not given proper maintenance. When a tool is used, it has to be maintained. People are the very same way. It's a very impersonal way of looking at it, but it's true: When you meet up with old friends, get together with a coworker at the bar, or even are called in to a meeting, maintenance is happening, one way or another. Knowing that this is true can help to lead you to a position where you can control the effectiveness of this maintenance.

Always appear to be more control of a situation than you are. We can never truly be the perfect mastermind of everything we aim to keep power over. Things will always go wrong. The difference between a professional and an amateur, though, is that the professional is always able to keep something out of sight long enough for it to be resolved by the people who ought to fix it. Sometimes it takes a real, noticeable distraction; while at others, it takes a small amount of sleight-of-hand or simply passively forcing a refocus on something else.

Talk about the other person. It sounds simple, doesn't it? But remember, people are selfish and you're a person, too. Talking almost explicitly about another person requires you to talk less about yourself. You'll have to step out of the spotlight and, instead, aim that pillar of white fluorescence at somebody else to gain their favor. Things not to do, however, are deflecting questions. If you're asked something about yourself, redirecting the question back to the asker or to somebody else does not imply that you're interested in them; it implies that you're trying to be secretive about your answer. Answer questions you're asked, but try to be on top of asking more questions than you answer. Follow up receiving answers with asking another question. If you do this, you will be able to not only make the other person feel as though you're interested in them, but will it will also give you control of the direction in which the conversation moves.

A pattern is easy to establish with the methods being taught: They're things people already do, passively, that you can wrestle control over actively. Mirroring is one such pattern. Passively, when encountering somebody whose presence we enjoy, we will mirror them. When we feel the other person is less than agreeable, we don't passively mirror them, but sometimes, you will need to cast your influence over others whose presence we could do without. Knowing what cues you need to follow to make somebody believe you thoroughly enjoy their presence are important to gaining influence over people.

Avoid taboo subjects, unless your goal is to extract taboo information. State politics, religion, financial situations, and sometimes family matters are subjects best left untouched, unless it's in a crowd where such things are acceptable. Family matters are acceptable to talk about with your family, religion within the church is acceptable, if regulated. Do not just avoid the taboo, however, but also the unprepared. If your goal in a conversation is not to be uneducated, make sure you're not walking blindly into a subject you don't know much about while debating somebody. To avoid this, you can do it with honesty by saying that you don't know much about the subject; or dishonestly, either by placing a false taboo around the subject, one that you don't truly feel, or by avoiding the subject through redirection; though remember - redirection implies lack of knowledge.

There is some merit to the idea that people teaching you something allows you to continue to gain influence over them. If you make yourself out to be the type of person who remains well educated and up-to-date, making a point to bring up current events as much as possible, it doesn't look good if/when something slips past unnoticed and you're left unprepared. That being said, though, if you keep yourself humble and stay slightly regulated with the news, people can feel a sense of importance that you can take into account when influencing them. People reveal much about themselves while they teach, and this can be useful information to you to take into account later on down the road. Take note of their words, the usage thereof, their body language, hand motions, all of it. Determine whether they are a closed speaker, one who does not use open body language when explaining things, or an open speaker who is often more aggressive, impactful, and speaks for longer stretches or more words without taking a pause to breathe. The ecstatic individuals are more likely to keep solid loyalties, while more reserved speakers are more critically thinking and will think more logically about who it is they trust. Both can be valuable assets for different reasons, though this mentality is important to note.

To wrap up this chapter, we're going to go over a few minor notes that are also essential to surviving in social situations. Eye contact is important, but don't hold it for too long. Remembering and referring to people by their names is more compassionate or caring than pronouns. People will notice if you remember their names or not. Physical contact is acceptable and even encouraged during the correct situations, but overdoing it can lead to awkward moments and negative memories. A good way to achieve influence is to work somebody down while they are tired. People are more susceptible to just about everything while they lack sleep, so arranging late-night meetings can help you achieve your goals with a slight amount of environmental behavior - but beware of the effects of late night meetings on your own physique.

Coming up, the use of reinforcement as a means of influence and what it can do to create patterns of loyalty and respect in the people you care most about.

Chapter 4: Reinforcement: Positive and Negative

The idea of reinforcement has long been a back-and-forth debate between famous psychologists. Modern day shrinks believe that positive reinforcement, which is the rewarding of good behavior and the rehabilitation of poor behavior, is the correct way to go about being influential. It is the primary way in which favor is gained, since it is the most natural way to go about things in a social situation: If you want people to listen to you, be nice to them, treat them well, and give them no reason to turn their backs on you. People are greedy, keep in mind. Positive reinforcement requires you to give something.

Negative reinforcement is the frowned-upon brother of positive reinforcement. It focuses solely on the bad things and seeks to punish for them. Things such as late arrival, missing due dates, or not being present for important meetings. These seek to punish, keep in mind, not necessarily to rehabilitate.

Yes, if somebody does something wrong and is punished for it, you can hope that they won't do it again - but they might. The upsides, however, are apparent: while its effectiveness is often called into question, it is a powerful tool after it is first applied. Recurring punishments wear down in potency over time, but the first time a salary is slashed or pain is dealt, it sticks with the person for some time. They will, however, eventually take the risk; this is almost certain.

In many environments, a combination of tactics is used. Sure, at work you might get a raise for good performance, but you can also get a cut for slacking off. In schools, a praise system is used for model behavior and a time-out is issued to those children who are acting out as bad examples. It is not always a double-edged sword, however. In today's society, the only reward you get for not breaking the law is living a normal life; and in the eyes of some people, being a regular citizen is a burden - mentally unstable felons don't have to vote, attend jury duty, or even be responsible for their own caretaking. Despite this, the United States Justice System is meant to appear less as a system of punishment, and more for one of rehabilitation. Despite this, the idea of going to prison and losing out on spending time with friends, family, loved ones, and possessions doesn't sound like a good time. While not intended to be viewed as punishment, prison time is still a form of negative reinforcement - and the alternative is not a reward in any monetary or physical sense.

So, what about using these tools for social purposes? What can you do to influence people using reinforcement? Well, of course, both kinds can be used - though often only the lighter side of the coin is utilized, and enforcing undesirable consequences can benefit you. In a public situation, punishing or implying punishment isn't received well by the people around you; this is a talk best saved one-on-one. Often, negative reinforcement is viewed in a bad light. Many think that blackmail is the only way to apply it, but this is far from the truth. If you lend out your car to a friend and give them gas money, and it is clear that they simply pocketed the cash, you can avoid immediate confrontation. Wait for them to ask again, deny them, and wait for them to ask why. Tell them you know that they pocketed the cash and say you want it back before they can have your car. Although a somewhat niche example, it can be applied across the board to many other situations of a similar caliber. Punishing or threatening punishment is far more than just blackmail.

But, what about positive reinforcement? It's true that this is the more popular of the two and for good reason: rewards are much easier to dish out in public than punishments, and doing so can even net you the respect of people around you.

Politicians don't hand off oversized novelty checks to charities in private - they give them out in public, but why? The reason they're handing the money off in the first place is because they want to appeal to the voter group which responds to that charity. Politicians want to look good in the eyes of the people who can put them in office and so they reward target demographics with all kinds of things - money to charities, legislation to restrict or loosen rules, or even the promise of a bailout in case things go wrong. They are positively reinforcing people who voted for them or promising to reward those who will vote. In smaller-scale deals, if somebody helps you or promises to help you, reward them for it. If your friend is bringing along people to help you move houses that you don't know, and you're looking to get them to help move your mom next month, give them food, provide cold drinks, and work the rest of your influential magic. And, in the classic case of pure positive influence, don't punish mistakes. Granted, depending on the situation, you can avoid that rule; but if you really need somebody to help you, and the mistake is minor, sweep it under the rug and let it stay in the past.

Rewards are not always items of value. Money or other coveted objects will do, sure, but sometimes, rewards can cost nothing. Physical reassurance, mental encouragement, and instilling a sense that listening to you is a good thing can all be rewarding enough for some. It is the intent of people to do well;

and if you can convince anybody that you do well, they will sometimes find this rewarding enough.

In the same vein, punishments can be mental, too. Berating somebody with an assault of words - either purposefully or in a flurry of emotion - can be all the punishment somebody needs to make an impression. This can work for you or against you - which is why control of your temper is important if you hope to make any lasting influence happen. A quick, unrelenting assault of words will not be perceived the same as a thought-out, intricate detailing of what they did wrong and why it is it upsets you so much. Insist that you're unsure if you can ever trust them again, or better yet reduce their importance in your social dealings and exclude them when it becomes possible and wait for them to apologize.

Reinforcement is another thing that is passively processed, though is made far more useful when applied actively. Knowingly deciding rewards and punishments for good jobs or wrongdoings is potent and crafty. Loyalty is sought after, while straying from the strongly recommended is a feat that will not land somebody within the circle of those you trust most. Deal the deck carefully and divide the treasures of your vault as you see fit, though keep in mind: rewards are a much better way to get people to like you, while the removal of trust or outright detriment of another person will make you seem less like a sound investment overall.

Chapter 4: Reinforcement: Positive and Negative

Chapter 5: Styles of Influence

When you think of influential people, what comes to mind? Not who, but what: what do the people do to be influential? Maybe they lead by example or instill their beliefs in others without necessarily practicing them. There are different ways one can go about being an influential person and each one appeals to different personality types. People don't often use more than one despite the fact that variety is what creates a compelling argument, and they don't consciously recognize the way that they do it at first. They're often told the way people believe they try to influence others. Utilizing multiple forms of persuasion can be a deadly tool when properly wielded and can be used to appeal to certain groups at certain times. The basic breakdown is as follows: people either use assertion, attempt to convince people to their viewpoint, employ negotiation tactics, build metaphorical bridges, or attempt to inspire others to follow in their wake. These five methods through which people influence others are approached in different ways and require different levels of aggression.

When asserting your standpoint, you typically address your idea or viewpoint as being correct and challenge others to prove you wrong. This method can be polarizing when presented to a wide audience and can create a feeling of "us or them." This is a useful method when one-on-one for this exact reason, since while it will help you garner the support of others, it might paint you in a negative light to others. If you win over the person you were originally trying to influence, those who took his side might not be so easily swayed. Keep a calm head and hammer away at the important parts of what you need to say.

Convincing is slightly different than assertion. When attempting to convince someone, it is much more focused on presenting support for your beliefs rather than staying steadfast in the face of deterrence. It's much more worthy of an intellectual debate and great at swaying crowds, which makes it more useful than assertion. Conceding while convincing is also far more acceptable and will damage you less than when you fold the hand while asserting your point. In one case, you're right and you believe it, and you want people to convert to what you believe without much struggle. Convincing somebody of something is an uphill battle.

Negotiation is something else that sounds similar as well, though these are not all synonyms. Negotiation is the only one of the two where you plan to give something up. When planning out a future for a house you want to build, and the person you will be living with tells you they don't like your idea of a fifty-foot indoor swimming pool, you can try to assert your position or convince them it's correct--or you can negotiate. Not fifty, but what about thirty? Maybe 20? 15? Even though you're giving some things up, the core idea of the indoor swimming pool stays the same. Do your best to prevent losses to the main soul of the prospect. If the swimming pool is no longer outside, or turns into a jacuzzi, you've lost. If it remains inside, and it is large enough to swim in, you've won. It's that simple. In negotiations, both sides can win, and both sides can lose. Due to the nature of negotiations themselves, they can be done with or as a group of people.

What's commonly called "bridge building" is the most widely used and accepted form in influence, since it's what you think of when you think about being influential. It's the building of relationships and establishing of groups of people aimed at one common goal - the thing that you're bridging towards. While this will be the most common way you gain influence, do not simply overlook the others. If you are standing on a platform, do not allow it to be whittled away at until nothing stands just because you're trying to repair a broken bridge. Sometimes, you need to stop and assert, convince, or negotiate your way through the gaps until somebody can fill them for you. To continue the metaphor, this takes the most work. While doing any of the previously mentioned, three can typically be employed in a single conversation, an argument, debate, or negotiation, although bridge building is a much longer process. It takes the upkeep of relationships, the recruitment for and creation of multiple bridges, and a solid idea of how strong the structure of your bridges are.

Finally, there is the concept of inspiring others in order to influence them. Inspiration is often a matter of ideals and goes hand-in-hand with honesty. A liar often finds it hard to influence people, while people who are honest or can maintain the illusion of honesty are able to be a source of information for many; and the inspired often find themselves following the example set by those who inspire them. Some are inspired to write due to an author or paint due to an artist, but these end goals likely aren't relevant to the way you want to influence others; you care more about inspiring them to your cause, and here's where honesty comes into play. If you can make your cause seem just and maintain honesty or an illusion thereof while doing it, people will be inspired by your noble causes to help you achieve them. Not everybody will be inspired by you, though, and this is certainly one of the hardest applications of influence due simply to the apathy of some. Some people don't want to get involved with the good causes of another since they're either dealing with their own noble causes, or are actually opposed to what you're doing. If you feel you can get them to help you, employing the other four styles can be effective to finally win them over and get them to see the goodness of your cause, allowing you to lead a larger following.

These are all the methods through which people influence others; and while a mixing and matching of different methods is often a more realistic approach, the five bases remain standing. Their use and application is important to take into consideration as you approach a period of time where you plan to influence people.

Chapter 6: A Warning

Being influential is dangerous. If you do it wrong, after long enough, you will lose the ability. There are many, many ways in which one can slip up and be caught off guard, knowing people will gladly step in to take your place and open the book to the marker you left it on. You don't want all your hard work to be squandered, and you certainly don't want somebody else to pick up the pieces you left behind. Detailed below are many, many ways in which your foresight can be blinded, your divinations false, and your very methods will be turned against you and used to tear down your magnificent palace of influence.

Play off your accomplishments. If you make it seem easier than they are, allow people to live in that fantasy. If you start telling people how it is you do what you do, you're begging to be replaced. Granted, some talents are natural and others are difficult to learn, but give people a way to be able to stab you in the back and take your place as though nothing happened, and they will not hesitate. If, however, you maintain

Chapter 6: A Warning

the idea that your gift is special and protected it through exclusivity, then by all means, let it be. You don't have to be simple, but you do have to make it look good.

Actions speak louder than words. In this case, you ought to be using both. The mere act of doing something isn't good enough. You have to tell people that you've done it. Don't work the angle too much on the same thing, but keep constantly working and improving it, and continually show people that you're doing it. Remember that the actions of the past become muted over time, so amplify them with refreshing new doings.

In conjunction with the last tip, never do too much. Yes, it is true that you must act in order for it to be loud; but when you set a goal for yourself, do not overachieve. If you work too hard, you'll pick up on the radar of many other people and end up with worse foes than you set out to defeat in the first place. If you decide to show your prowess, and overexert yourself, the results will seem to be gleaming until you look at the other "rewards" that seem like they were dredged out of a stagnant riverbed. It is not worth it.

The other consequence of overworking is one related to superiors. If you work too hard, sure, they'll benefit from it at first; but they will begin to think ahead and be reminded of somebody else who worked hard enough at something to get well rewarded - themselves. They aren't usually the first to have had the position they're working in and they aren't looking to be replaced by somebody working under them. Do your job, maybe do it better than anybody else; but do your best not to be an outlier, and certainly don't use your boss's old turnouts as a goal to set.

Do not be forgettable. Don't take this as being ostentatious, either. This is not in a physical sense; this is in a mental one. Wear the right clothes, do your hair properly, maybe a slight oddity in the tie or cufflinks when dressing formal is good; but overall, you don't want to be weird looking, just memorable, and all of that is a matter of thinking. Act eccentric; don't dress it. Whatever you can do to make people remember you: do it. You want to be on their minds as much as possible, especially when not directly in front of them.

Do not allow anybody you wanted out of the picture back in again. If you do anything to assist those you wanted gone, be it out of pity or spite, they will get back at you for it. If you truly seek to annihilate somebody, don't leave anything left of them. Mending the wound of the man you stabbed in the back will only put him close enough to you to do the same when you turn yours.

Things can absolutely be too good to be true. We learn this one by ourselves; but at this point, it ought to become a hatred. If something really does look like it'll take little work with

Chapter 6: A Warning

major payout, don't buy into it. Anybody selling snake oil wants you to ignore the asterisk next to the product details, and anybody you don't know who's giving out free advice has ulterior motives that may or may not be trying to cause your downfall.

You have to be needed. The moment people don't need you, you're out. Do your best to keep yourself relevant. If people no longer depend on you and can rely on themselves to do your job, you're done for. If it's inevitable and they plan to have somebody else teach them to do your job, you have two options: let them, or make it painful. If you let them, you're accepting defeat and moving on, which sometimes is the better option. It lets you get a head start on finding somewhere else and getting new people to depend on you. If they ask you to teach it, instead, you can overwhelm them and try to maintain your usefulness. Unnecessary jargon, complicated explanations, and other such tactics can help to possible cancel the process.

The hearts and minds of the people must remain pure; and to do this, any threat to their mental stability has to be silenced or removed early on before it can spread. A chain is only as strong as its weakest link; and when that tears, you lose it all. If one link of the chain is rusting, it could infect others and multiple weak links is a chain even more likely to break. If you have a team pointed at a goal and a naysayer sprouts up in the group, silence them early before their ill will can contaminate anybody else. Encourage anybody who has questions to see you to voice any concerns they may have.

Know weakness. It comes in many forms and hides in many ways. If people do not hide their weakness, because they do not have to, then it is not of great importance to them - it doesn't matter much. A weakness is a secret, something that they can't have shown to the outside world. If our weaknesses could be exposed openly, then they should be. The weaknesses that are hidden hold the most weight. They cut deepest, when exposed. These things, we all have them. The key is to identify them. Figure them out. For your own sake, and for the sake of others. Sometimes, weaknesses aren't controllable actions, they're habits or other such things, compulsory. Create your own armor and examine it as you would that of others. You don't have to expose or even use weaknesses, but know it for every person you think you need to - and everybody else as well.

CHAPTER 6: A WARNING

Chapter 7: Influence on TV and in Real Life

Providing a real-world example of these influential aspects is easy to do when one looks to television. Advertisers are influencing you always, in many ways. Selling you a product, an idea, or persuading your vote, advertisements are trying to get into your head and manipulate you in the most one-sided way ever: for them to manipulate you, all you have to do is listen to their words. For you to do it to them, an alternate method of communication has to be established, be it over the phone, by writing a letter, or with an in-person meeting; and most people don't contact the directors or targets of advertisers - they just watch them.

We'll start with commercial ads, since they are the most common year-round. The people put in charge of commercial ads have a goal to sell you whatever it is they were paid to sell you; their agenda is purely financial. That being said, the reason for them to want try to influence you is almost always because of being rewarded with something--this is the cause. Sometimes, incredibly rarely, advertisers will enjoy a product and offer their services firsthand - but they never do it for free. Large companies have no need for freelance advertisers; they create a department dedicated to it.

Commercial adverts can be more than just assertive. Sometimes, they do not address any counterclaim and have one directive: to tell you where to spend your money. You can't negotiate with a television, of course, and you also can't build a metaphorical bridge to one; but it is a possibility for them to convince you through simulating a debate, pretending to give you back-and-forth on a subject. These are often comedically one-sided, however, such as the famous "Mac and PC" advertisements put out by Apple several years ago. It's also possible for an advertisement to inspire, though often, commercial ads do not attempt to do this. This is the method political ads often employ.

Political advertisements can take on a plethora of methods through which they try to influence you. Some are assertive, speaking of the goodness of one candidate or the negative impact of another, while another approach to these commercials can be focused on trying to convince you of something, telling of a candidate's golden idea of the future and prosperity in the position they plan to fill. Political advertisements can also inspire, as mentioned earlier, and these types are usually trying to remind a person of all the good things the person in question has done in the past. You can normally only do this if the candidate had been on the news in the past for something they've done that has positively impacted their community.

The incentive behind political adverts is normally more than just a monetary reward, though these, too, are important to those planning them. A candidate's PR department sets an agenda for the advertising team and tells them how to do the ad. In essence, their job is to create a candidate who has no downsides and shall do nothing wrong, and paint the opposition as somebody who will mess up or be defeated in their purpose.

But, what about other real-life examples? What about corporate meetings, friendly get-togethers, and other such activities? Well, remember, they're all maintenance. But, that being said, while maintenance is being performed, there's always room for upgrades. People are always trying to influence you, no matter who it is. Be it recommending bands, trying to instill new business plans, or just trying to get you on their side in a hot debate over a small pointless triviality. No matter what, you and other people are constantly battling for influence, and it's often more of a trade or an exchange. It is possible to have total influence over another, though that often is not the case.

Normally, your goal is to be more influential than any other person; to get what you want however it is you decide to get it. Standing steadfast, convincing, negotiating, building relationships, and being a model of inspiration are all the ways in which you can influence others; however, these same ways are going to be the way people influence you. Watch out for how it is they're approaching the matter and counter their methods as best you can. You want to be more influential than anybody else, normally, as that is part of the matter.

In the real world, never forget that often times the people you want to influence aren't those you have to worry too intently about making a mistake when near. You can easily afford to make some mistakes, especially early on, so don't stress the idea of perfection when you're just starting. Often times, you can play off any mistake as just a passive misstep, since to rehash that which has already been said many times before, all it is you do when you influence people is perhaps be a little more aggressive than normal with your points; but primarily, you're utilizing actions that are normally passive and making them active. This means that when you make a mistake, it will often be difficult to tell; but you can always easily make anything seem accidental.

In this way, be bold! Aim for the moon here! Confidence is key and don't let the guidelines restrict you too much. If you play it too close to the book, you'll end up sounding more like it than yourself. Don't let anything diminish your personality, since it is the most important part of influencing somebody. Nobody wants to follow a programmable person; they want to follow somebody who is able to adapt and mold their actions based on information and current ideology.

A few final notes before we reach the conclusion that will help you better apply yourself in everything you do: dress for the occasion. Know what you need to wear for the appropriate where. Location is everything for this and you should notice that you can tell almost every time what you need to wear based on the location in which it's going to be. If you know where it is to be hold, and you have advanced notice a little bit of information about the locale, you can tell how exactly you'll need to dress.

Not just the way you dress, but also the way you look is important. This is a hard one to give good advice on as it changes from place-to-place. If you're a businessman, short, gelled hair and a business coat look good. If you're trying to look impressive as the leader of a local cult, brown robes tied with a frayed rope is the classic look that never fails to impress, despite its cliché nature. All jokes aside, considering this isn't a guide on fashion, it really is hard to tell you how you ought to look on a casual, normal basis when interacting with people who you need to impress; but one tip that never fails is mirroring. As long as you're on par with somebody else, you can always copy their look, albeit with some adjustments, of course.

Finally, the last point to be made about real life influence: don't get too into it. It's real life being discussed here and while being influential is truly an important part of it, stay grounded. Playing crazy head games and isolating ideas and attacking people for ideals can paint you in a negative light. The key to being influential is to play the game casually. Don't get overly involved, and more than anything else, don't forgot who you are, what your goals are, and what you've already gotten done. Cheers, and good luck out there.

Chapter 7: Influence on TV and in Real Life

Conclusion

I'm happy you read through to the end of *How to Influence People*, and I hope it was an informative piece, able to provide you with the tools you need to achieve your goals and ambitions.

The next step is to go out and put this knowledge to the test. Step up and try it out. It will take a small amount of trial and error, but the beauty of social situations is that it is always easy to save face. If you make a mistake, it can be covered over easily enough. Never forget the number one rule: people are greedy. If you want to influence them, the words on the previous pages can be summed up simply: prey upon greed. Whether the greed is about money, politics, or reciprocity, people can be influenced. Your friends will be less greedy, perhaps even selfless, though they often don't have to be influenced nearly as much as coworkers and strangers.

Conclusion

Finally, if you found this book useful in anyway, a review on Amazon is always appreciated! Thank you so much again; now get out there and start influencing!

CONCLUSION

Finally, if you found this book useful in anyway, a review on Amazon is always appreciated. Thank you so much and I know you'll kick out there and kill it my friend!

Free Preview: How Analyzing People Helps you

If you found this book helpful, you might also be interested in my other book *How to Analyze People*. In this free preview chapter, you will learn how analyzing people can help you in different situations. You will quickly see how analyzing people is the perfect complementary skill to influencing people. *How to Analyze People* is now available on Amazon. Never stop to learn, never stop to improve! That's how you succeed and outperform your competition!

Chapter 1: How Analyzing People Helps You

Although you may find this topic intriguing, you might wonder how this knowledge can be of practical use in your life. To put it simply, a whole new world of possibilities opens up to you when you learn how to read the behavior and feelings of others. Situations that once threw you into a confused state of mind with seemingly no way out will no longer be an issue for you. Dealing with "difficult" people will no longer be a source of stress and misinterpreting the wants and needs of others won't mystify you anymore.

Successful People are already Aware of this Power:

People who enjoy successful love lives, profitable money situations, and careers already know all about the life-changing and critical power of analyzing others confidently. However, this pursuit is not always so easy. For some of us, this is not an intuitive skill, and most people find that they have to study it quite intently to begin getting a grasp on the subject.

Anyone can Learn this Skill:

The great news here is that all people can learn the hacks, tricks, and skills needed for becoming great with reading and analyzing others. The incredible power behind seeing what a person is truly thinking can be gained by any person who discovers the secrets of analyzing others.

What are the Consequences of not Learning this?

- **Job Complications:** When you are unaware of how to read others, you are more likely to run into conflict at work. If you have ever wondered why your boss seems to have it in for you, or why you can't seem to make yourself clear to your co-workers, this information will help you immensely.

- **Personal Relation Problems:** Without knowing how to read your partner, a healthy and happy relationship is impossible. You will likely find that fights last a lot longer than they should, or that you simply don't know how to fix problems when they arise until you learn this valuable skill. Do you get into fights with your spouse and stop halfway through to realize that you don't know what you're fighting about or how to solve the problem? This can be helped by learning how to analyze others.

- **Trouble Understanding yourself:** True analysis of human behavior does not just entail reading others, but also knowing how to read ourselves. To be frank, without understanding yourself, life is going to be a struggle for you. And there is little to no hope of learning how to read other people if you haven't first figured out how to understand and read your own feelings and thoughts. Since this is a key factor in learning to analyze people, we will cover this in depth in the last chapter of the book.

The foundation of unlocking true connections with people, personal success, and real happiness is yours to take as soon as you become aware of some simple factors of body language and basic psychology. You can free yourself from the inherent limits of everyday communication by understanding the world in a deeper way. Don't allow yourself to be held back by your inability to read others.

How to Approach this Information:

Before you can gain benefits to knowing the information you are about to be given in this book, you need to know how to approach it correctly. Here are some considerations to keep in mind:

- **Use Observation plus Experience:** Although skills of observation are valuable and absolutely necessary when it comes to analyzing people, they won't be of much value to you unless you combine it with personal experience. This combination will aid you in learning to tell personalities and types of people apart from one another. It's impossible to take one single formula and apply it to every person or even their every trait.

- **Humans are Complex:** Knowing more than others about analysis of behavior will put you miles ahead of other people, but keep in mind that humans are complex beings. There is not a simple method for knowing everything about everyone, all the time. And any approach to learning more about this takes time and effort. Like any other skill, it takes patience and practice.

- **Interaction helps you Learn more:** Gaining conceptual knowledge through reading about a topic, for example, is helpful in learning about any given subject. But interacting with people is another great way to learn how to interpret them. This can involve eating with the person at a restaurant or simply going out for a walk. During this activity, you can keep a close eye on their mannerisms, how patient they are, as well as their general temperament.

  Being in either a casual or professional situation with someone else will help you understand the way they function in various scenarios, along with how they normally act on a day to day basis. You can supplement this general observation with strategies about whether they prefer to work as a team or on their own, and to test their factual awareness.

- **Try not to Assume:** Although it's nice to learn how to read other people, it's important not to assume too much. Although you may get quite good at interpreting how others feel and the thoughts they think, it's always best to check for confirmation before you assume anything for sure. Look for multiple clues, including context and past behavior, in order to form a solid opinion and then try to test this by asking them for confirmation or observing their behavior to see if you were right.

It's about Knowledge, not Judgment:

Don't mistake the art of getting to know the thoughts and habits of others as a way of judging their character. Along the way, you will learn how to interpret other people, but don't allow other people to judge your willingness to learn or know. This is a good habit to form, one that can help you stay aware of the personality types constantly surrounding us in daily life. All people are ultimately different from one another; but by gaining understanding of them, we widen our perspective and abilities in general.

End of the free preview chapter

If you are interested in learning more about how to analyze people, get yourself a copy of the book on Amazon!

www.ingramcontent.com/pod-product-compliance
Lightning Source LLC
Chambersburg PA
CBHW061207180526
45170CB00002B/993